The 7 Simple Steps to Mindset Mastery

SCOTT CAPELIN

Business Mentor and Consultant, Bachelor of Commerce Degree, Wellness and Lifestyle Coach, International Business Franchisor, Nutritionist, Personal Trainer, Pilates Instructor, NLP Practitioner

The 7 Simple Steps to Mindset Mastery

Copyright © 2022 by Scott Capelin
Book Layout © 2022 by Evolve Global Publishing
www.inlifecoaching.com.au

This is the part where the book normally says "All rights reserved", and you can't use any of it or reproduce it without the authors permission. I don't care about that. Knock yourself out. If you can use something from this book to help yourself or help someone else, go for it.

Limit of Liability Disclaimer: The information contained in this book is for information purposes only and may not apply to the reader's situation. The author, publisher, distributor and provider offer no warranty about the content or accuracy of content enclosed. The information provided is subjective. Keep this in mind when reviewing this guide. Neither the publisher nor the author shall be liable for any loss of profit or any other commercial damages resulting from the use of this guide. All links are for information purposes only and are not warranted for content, accuracy or any other implied or explicit purpose.

All statements and opinions are those of the respective authors. Content has been provided by the authors under a non-exclusive license, and the authors are solely responsible for the content in their respective chapters. The publisher will not be held liable for any content provided by the authors.

Earnings Disclaimer: All income examples in this book are just that – examples. They are not intended to represent or guarantee that everyone will achieve the same results. Each individual's success will be determined by his or her desire, dedication, background, effort and motivation to work. There is no guarantee anyone will duplicate any of the results stated here. Any business endeavour has inherent risk or loss of capital.

Trademarks: All product names, logos, and brands are the property of their respective owners. All company, product, and service names used in this book are for identification purposes only. The use of these names, logos, and brands does not imply endorsement. All other trademarks cited herein are the property of their respective owners.

This book is not intended as a substitute for medical advice. The reader should regularly consult a physician in matters relating to his/her health and particularly with respect to any symptoms that may require diagnosis or medical attention.

Fit to Flourish
The 7 Simple Steps to Mindset Mastery
First Edition, 2023
ISBN: 978-0-6454380-6-2 (Amazon Print)
ISBN: 978-0-6454380-3-1 (IngramSpark Paperback)
ISBN: 978-0-6454380-4-8 (IngramSpark Hardcover)
ISBN: 978-0-6454380-5-5 (Smashwords)
ASIN: B0BTP38SRS (Amazon Kindle)
ISBN: 978-0-6454380-5-5 (e-Book)
Author Website: www.scottcapelin.co
Main Website: www.inlifecoaching.com.au
Publisher Website: www.evolveglobalpublishing.com

Table of Contents

Dedication 7

Introduction 9

Step One: Values, Vision, and Vitality 17

Step Two: Gratitude, Growth, and Goals 37

Step Three: Passion, Purpose, and Positivity.. 53

Step Four: Conviction, Connection, and Contribution................................ 65

Step Five: Strength, Self-Image, and Surrender 75

Step Six: Faith, Fulfilment, and Focus 87

Step Seven: Affirmations, Abundance and Action 97

Final Thoughts... 109

About the Author.. 111

Scott Capelin

Dedication

This book is dedicated to anyone who has an intuitive feeling that life can be richer and more enjoyable, more fun, and more fulfilling. This book is designed for people who feel that life is short, so we might as well have a go, be playful, and spend time pursuing our passions. On the other hand this book is for those who feel that life is plenty long enough to become the best versions of ourselves, and to experience all the joy, beauty and abundance we can squeeze from our years on this planet. This book is for people who don't want to settle for average.

This book aims to inspire you to flourish and live your best and fullest life. Hopefully some of the thoughts in these pages can open your heart and mind, take you from confusion to clarity, motivate you to take action, and make you believe that anything is possible. It is the author's hope that this book makes you aware that you are stronger than you know, and that you can do anything and get through anything, and that all the good stuff lies on the other side of your comfort zone.

Scott Capelin

Introduction

Flourishing! There's something about this word that brings to mind a garden full of life, beauty, strength, happiness, fulfilment, and peace. It's a place of harmony and abundance, where you are thriving! Most people have some image in their minds of a flourishing life –where you are fit, happy, and love your life! However, this is not always the case. Sometimes, life can be a garden full of weeds.

We hear the word "Mindset" a lot. What does it really mean? Defining "mindset" can be broad and vague and, it becomes easy to dismiss. What kind of mindset would you like to live with? How do you want to see your life and the world? How do you deal with challenges? Can you see the gift in every situation – even the bad ones? Do you think you are a positive person? Or do you automatically think about what could go wrong every time you hear a new idea? Are you excited about the day ahead, the week ahead, and the decade ahead? Do you live with an attitude of gratitude, or do you focus on the things you don't have? Do you have goals and a sense of purpose in your life? Are you growing as a person, or do you feel stagnant and in a rut? Are you surrounded by people who lift you up and inspire you to be better? Do you have a sense of hope and faith about the future, and a belief that everything is unfolding perfectly for you? Do you look for the best in yourself and others? The answers to all these questions tie into the health of your mindset.

We live in a time where anxiety and depression are everywhere. Would you believe 84% of people don't like their work? 40% of marriages fail. Half the western world is overweight or obese. And it's getting worse. We wonder, *did I miss the day at school when they taught us how to live our best lives?* Why weren't we taught to think to be the best version of ourselves? They taught us to play the recorder, and how to square dance. We all had to wear the same uniform. We had to sit down and stand up when the bell rang. We had to study English and Maths, but not how to look after ourselves. How do you budget properly? How do you have a great relationship? How do I open a small business?

The other day, I discovered something interesting. If you type into Google, "How to learn…", one of the top three predictive text answers globally is, "How to learn to love myself." Millions of people are searching for the answers to happiness and fulfilment, and how to build their self-esteem.

Living inside your own head is an interesting place. You are the only person who you have to live with 24/7. We have seven times more conversations with ourselves than everyone else in our life combined, so we need to make our minds a safe, happy, strong, and inspiring place. We need our self-talk to be uplifting and positive. That's the reason I named this book "Fit to Flourish." Being physically fit and healthy is only one part of flourishing. Another part is mindset. It's beneficial to be strong physically, mentally, emotionally, and spiritually. Mindset is so important to flourishing. Every moment of every day we think thoughts that shape our every action and every response. Our thoughts determine how we feel. How we feel determines the vibration we put out into the universe. And the vibration we emit is responsible for what we attract. Look at everything in your life right now – look at the areas you think are good and the things you consider to be bad. Everything is a result of how you think.

The problem is that we are our own worst critics. We can make progress and then self-sabotage. Suppose that, instead of focusing on internal criticism, we focus instead on qualities that result in the optimal mindset? How would your life look if your mind responded every time in the best way possible to point you towards a flourishing life, rather than criticising you?

There's a book called "Mans Search for Meaning" by Viktor Frankl, a psychologist who found himself in a concentration camp during World War II. He observed many external factors were affecting the people in the camps. There they were, surrounded by the daily horror of the holocaust. They couldn't control what was happening, but they could control how they thought about what was happening.

I want to be clear. It's not about being positive all the time. Life isn't always rosy. Life is full of glorious moments, and terrible lows. Life is full of short-term shocks. There's only one constant in life, and that is change. Your mood and your state are a bit like a gauge on a petrol tank. Sometimes it's full; sometimes it's empty. We can't just cover up a bad day with a smile and think positively out of it.

This book is about giving you the tools to help acknowledge your empty gauge days and bounce back quickly. It's about how to react proactively to those days and get back onto an even keel. Happiness can't be conditional on external events. If that were the case, we would be at the mercy of things beyond our control. If we're only happy and positive when things are going our way, then we won't be happy all that much, will we? And we will be very susceptible to regular disappointment.

Most people walk around thinking that happiness is the goal of life. But how long does that last? When you look at things on a deeper level, you may realise the goal of life is actually about fulfilment. It's about being at peace with yourself. When you're at peace with yourself and what's happening around you, everything else just takes care of itself.

You can't change the thoughts, actions, or decisions of other people around you. And despite our best efforts, those closest to us have an enormous influence on our thinking.

Do you remember the saying, "Grant me the serenity to accept the things I can't change, the courage to change the things I can, and wisdom to know the difference"? Then why do we get upset at the weather, or who won the election? These are things we cannot change.

Robin Sharma says that the secret of happiness is simple. Find out what you love to do, then direct all your energy towards doing it. The happiest, healthiest, most satisfied people around have found their passion, and spend every day pursuing it. I want to walk you through the seven steps to building a mindset to help you become fit to flourish. Listed below is a summary of the steps, and the rest of this book is dedicated to explaining each part of the process in a little more depth. This is a not a long book. You could read it on one or two sittings. It's designed to be that way, so you don't get bored. I encourage you to think about each element presented here and question it; challenge it. Is it relevant for you? What's your take on it? Do you see the value in it?

Here we go!

Step One: Vision, Values, and Vitality! One of our primary aims here is to develop a vision for your life and the person you want to be. We identify your personal core values as a human being. And we discuss how to live with vitality! Once you have a sharp vision and a deep understanding of you own personal core values, we dig deeper into your "why" and we discover what motivates you, and what drives you to achieve your best life? From here you are perfectly positioned to make life decisions that are beautifully aligned with what's most important to you.

Step Two: Gratitude, Goals, and Growth. Cultivate an attitude of gratitude in your life. Being thankful is the healthiest of human emotions. It directly opposes negative thoughts and helps to build your mindset. It's the ultimate antidote to negativity, because you can't be grateful and fearful at the same time. You can't be simultaneously grateful and jealous. You can't be grateful and negative. Gratitude is an attractive quality, and it makes you shine. Think about how unappealing ingratitude and arrogance are! And you tend to get more of what you are grateful for! Try to look for the gift in every situation. In this section we also discuss personal and professional growth, and how all the beauty, joy, and abundance in life lies outside your comfort zone. We also discuss goal setting, which drives determination, eliminates distraction, and provides direction.

Step Three: Passion, Purpose, and Positivity! Doesn't that sound good? Can you spend your days radiating positivity? Are you the kind of person that other people want to be around? Don't allow a negative weed to grow inside the garden of your mind. You really can choose your attitude! You have the power and the ability to choose how you react to events happening around you. And following on from Step Two, we link our goals with a deep sense of purpose.

Step Four: Conviction, Connection, and Contribution. Here we start to tie everything together as we build on our vision, values, goals, and purpose, which results in a powerful sense of conviction. In addition to that we explain why connection is one of the most basic yet strongest human needs, and we uncover why meaningful connections to people, places, or vocations result in deep satisfaction. When we contribute to the world on a larger scale it brings fulfilment into our lives. We tend to derive the most fulfilment when we serve others. If you're not fulfilled, you're probably not making a difference.

Step Five: Strength, Self-Image, and Surrender. The focus here is how to build mental strength, be a resilient person, and have a positive self-image. In times of greatest challenge, it is these areas that can make a difference. It is here we also look at surrender and what it is. It's not abandoning goals. It's letting go of resistance, and the emotional struggle to attain our goals. As Wayne Dyer said, "Be open to everything and attached to nothing."

Step Six: Faith, Fulfilment, and Focus. This is where we get a little spiritual. You don't have to be religious to embrace a deep sense of faith that the world is a friendly place and that things are always working out for you. It's important to have faith and hope. In this step we also define the fundamental areas of focus in your life in order for you to live with maximum fulfilment.

Step Seven: Affirmations, Abundance, and Action! Affirmations are phrases we can say to ourselves to embed positive beliefs into our mind and increase uplifting self-talk and quash niggling doubts. Motivation results from an action; it's not the cause of it. Does that make sense? People think they will take action when they become motivated. It's the opposite – take some action and you start to build motivation! We become more motivated and inspired after we have acted! If you wait around to become motivated before you've taken action, you could literally be waiting forever! Many people don't know where to begin, so they simply don't, and they stay stuck in life. People may not take action due to fear of the unknown, or fear of failure. A mindset of abundance, believing that anything is possible, believing that there is plenty of help available, and believing that there is enough for everyone can help work through the challenges in taking the action required to make the changes required to live our best lives. Once we have our mindset right, taking action towards our flourishing life becomes easier.

Scott Capelin

Step One: Values, Vision, and Vitality

Scott Capelin

The starting point of our journey is to create the foundation for an improved mindset. When we live our lives aligned with our values, pursuing a vision for our life, and exercising and eating to create vitality in our bodies, you will see an immediate positive change.

Values

Fit to Flourish encourages a deep understanding of who you are. This starts with knowing your values. I have always felt that the greatest gift you can give yourself, and those around you, is the gift of self-awareness. Your values shape your whole life, what you enjoy, what you don't like, what you think, and what you do. What you value is what you focus on. It's what you pursue. It points you to what your best life looks like.

Why are values important? When you understand your values, you can take steps to live in alignment with them. Each step takes you closer to a life of fulfilment, a life of meaning, a flourishing life. Your values are the foundation upon which you have built your life. These are the dreams we had as children, the qualities of our character, even what we do for leisure or enjoyment. Quite simply, if you live your life on track with the things that are most important to you, you will be happy. Conversely, if you spend most of your time doing things that aren't a core part of your nature, you will be unhappy.

The problem is that many people don't spend time in activities that line up with their values. Many times I've helped people fill in a time log of their week and found that people spend up to 80% of their time doing things they don't like. Sounds miserable, doesn't it? Some people are a little depressed in life, and sometimes it's because they're misaligned with their values. Or maybe they don't have things to look forward to, and we cover this more in the next section when we discuss Goals. They survive the week, reach Friday, and feel relieved that they've reached the weekend. They hang out for their four weeks off each year (two of which often aren't even in their control; they need to take them when the business closes for Christmas). Why should you allow someone to tell you when you can take time off? And why can someone dictate what your time is worth?

> **Values are like fingerprints.
> Nobodies are the same, but you leave
> them all over everything you do.**
>
> - Elvis Presley

Differences in values between people can even contribute to arguments. Especially when two people are looking at the same situation through the lenses of their different values. It's worth remembering that we cannot control what anyone else does, says, thinks, or feels, so it is rarely worth trying to change their opinion.

On the other hand, there's a philosophy that when we don't like someone, it's usually because they remind us of something in ourselves we don't like. If you're ever upset with somebody because of something they've done, ask yourself, have you ever done something similar? Have you ever been secretive? Have you ever cheated or taken a shortcut? Have you ever not told the truth? Can you truly get upset with someone when you've done something like it? It is important that we acknowledge and take ownership of these less desirable qualities in ourselves.

Science in the past century has delved deeply into what life looks like on the sub-atomic and quantum levels. Scientists have discovered that everything is simply energy. The atoms which make up your body are protons and electrons spinning. Solid matter is nothing more than the energy of one surface reacting to the energy of another. This carries down into the quantum level, where protons and electrons themselves are made of different energy.

Why is that important? When energy makes up the basis of everything, then the energy we radiate becomes so important. Compare two people. One person is miserable in his or her job and home, depressed and anxious. They give off different energy to the person who lives a full life of fulfilment and abundance. We all know someone who is just draining to be around, and often we can't say why.

It's hard to be that person radiating positivity and abundance when you're mostly doing things you don't love. If you don't like your job, how are you going to be a beacon of positivity 24/7? And if you are not emitting a positive aura, from a law of attraction perspective you will struggle to draw anything positive towards you.

Have you ever set a goal, achieved it, and felt nothing? Almost like the achievement was meaningless? This is usually because the goal you set doesn't align with your values. Perhaps it wasn't in line with your values when you started. Perhaps your values shifted. Perhaps it's in line with some of your values, but there's a mismatch between the importance of the goal and the importance of the value. For example, say you work extremely hard to earn a promotion at work. This is an important goal necessary for providing for your family and pursuing your career, but the mismatch comes along because spending time with your family is a more important value than getting a pay rise which requires you to work even harder.

An important question in this journey is "What are your values?" There are some simple steps to discover your values. I often collaborate with clients using a time log, examining where they spend most of their time, but also where that time feels most fulfilling. Where do you focus your thoughts? Where do you spend your money? What do you spend your time dreaming about?

If you want to know where your heart is, look where your mind goes when it wanders.

A wonderful way to discover your values is to ponder this scenario: You have two years to live; you're in perfect health; you have unlimited resources—how do you spend your time? What do you do? These questions leave clues to what you value. It tells you what's most important to you in life.

Not knowing your values is a recipe for feeling unfulfilled. You are stumbling around from day to day in a blur as days turn into weeks and weeks turn into years. Soon you feel you haven't made the most of the last decade or so. Depression affects one in five people in their life. We all know someone who struggles with it. It's a plague on our society and can strike anyone in the prime of life. They may look like they have it all together—a high-paying job, a good relationship—but they secretly struggle with depression or anxiety. Sometimes, it could be because they aren't positively affecting the world around them.

Most likely it's a lack of alignment with their values that hasn't been acknowledged or addressed.

As humans, we have six basic needs, but the one that ranks highest is contribution. Your success, fulfilment, and happiness directly relate to the value you add to the world. It doesn't take much. You could volunteer at a homeless shelter or coach a local kids sporting team. Better still, your work will have a positive impact on the community around you.

> **Success, like happiness, cannot be pursued. It must ensue. And it only does so as the unintended side effect of one's personal dedication to a cause greater than oneself.**
>
> - Viktor Frankl

The key is to do something. Anthony Robbins loves to say, "Emotion is energy in motion." It's hard to be highly energetic and depressed at the same time. When you do something that focuses on helping others, it helps create positive energy. This brings out the positive emotion in you.

I want to clarify that depression is usually not something you can just snap out of. Medical professionals should support a journey out of depression. Emotional trauma needs counselling, and medication can assist chemical imbalances. Taking a step to get help could be the step you take. Once you're on that journey, you take another action, and another.

When you are in alignment with who you are, you can't help but lift those around you. As you discover your five top values in life, you shape your contribution and your activities around those values.

There are hundreds of values, but some of the common values include:

- Family
- Gratitude
- Health
- Finances
- Career
- Business
- Travel
- Freedom
- Fun

- Appreciation
- Joy
- Harmony
- Creativity

To discover what your values are, look for the things in life that you don't need to be motivated to do. If you research and book your holidays a year in advance, travel is probably a high value. If you spend half of your Sunday working on your business, then business probably a high value for you. If you spend every spare moment with your family, then that's probably a high value of yours. If you find it hard to save money, stop beating yourself up. It's probably not a high value. Don't do it because someone else says you should.

Some time ago, I worked with a lovely, bubbly, super-intelligent young woman called Christie. She is an amazing person! Her parents, like many, wanted to see her in a secure career, making good money. Being accountants, they pushed her to study accounting and become an accountant. Now there's nothing wrong with being an accountant if it lines up with your values. They loved her deeply and wanted her to be financially secure (there's a hint about what they valued).

The problem was that Christie was deeply passionate about music. She was miserable as an accountant. That misery led her into depression. All she wanted to do was focus on her creativity and music, but didn't want to let her parents down. Those two values (creativity and family) were competing to be expressed in her life. She highly valued family and wanted to make her parents happy and respected them. She, however, could not express her value of creativity as a major part of her life. This was creating deep emotional conflicts within her. Unresolved conflicts that were emerging as anxiety and an eating disorder.

Open and honest communication could have resolved this challenging situation. The value of family was stronger than the value of creativity, so Christie didn't talk about these issues, internalising them instead.

> My father could have been a great comedian, but he didn't believe that was possible for him, and so he made a conservative choice. Instead, he got a safe job as an accountant. When I was 12 years old, he was let go from that safe job, and our family had to do whatever we could to survive. I learned many great lessons from my father, not the least of which was that you can fail at what you don't want, so you might as well take a chance on doing what you love.
>
> - Jim Carrey

Vision

Vision can be hard to define, but it's more than just a goal, dream, or idea. It's more of a driving force that lines up with what you value. It needs to be inspiring. Your vision is a picture of a life where you live with an intense sense of purpose. Your vision is like a compass that keeps guiding you in a certain direction.

To aid you in defining your vision, you can create a vision statement. This is a document that lays out a vision for your life. It's a bit like creating a dream world for you to live in. You can put together a vision statement in a four-step process:

1. Outline the major areas in life: your career, health, social life, and recreation.
2. Write in bullet points of things you DON'T want in each area.
3. Here you write out what you DO want in each area. Write the opposite of everything in the point above.
4. Write the points you want into a story describing your ideal life. Write it in the first person in the present tense. e.g.: I live a life with an amazing body shape and elevated levels of energy.

It can end up reading like this: I wake up each day feeling energetic and grateful! Healthy eating and exercising is part of my lifestyle that I enjoy and comes easily to me. I have more money than I need! My relationship with my partner is loving, honest, and exciting! We travel the world each year to amazing destinations!

It's that simple. That vision statement can be so inspiring, especially when read out daily. It becomes your compass, keeping you pointed in the right direction by reminding you of the life you want to create.

Reminding you of the life that's important to you and your values.

Doesn't that sound great? These can also be considered to be affirmations, which we cover in the last section of this book.

> **If you do follow your bliss you put yourself on a kind of track that has been there all the while, waiting for you, and the life that you ought to be living is the one you are living. When you can see that, you begin to meet people who are in the field of your bliss, and they open the doors to you. I say, follow your bliss and don't be afraid, and doors will open where you didn't know they were going to be.**
>
> - Joseph Campbell

Your vision statement is usually a long-term vision for your life, from which you draw your short-term activities and goals. Some call the long-term vision a BHAG; a big hairy audacious goal. Your vision statement can include all the big dreams you have in your life. It could be to build an orphanage in Cambodia, travel the world, run a marathon, or to live in a certain house in a certain location.

Ultimately, the idea is to manifest your vision. Everything happens twice; first in your mind, and then in reality. We are trying to carve our vision into our subconscious mind, so we make aligned, inspired decisions and take steps towards living our ideal life. When we know our values, and we have a vision for our life, it becomes so much easier to make decisions that line up with that vision.

When you make those decisions, you gain conviction. Conviction leads to self-assurance. Self-assurance becomes independence. Independence becomes an aura of confidence. And an aura of confidence can be one of the sexiest things alive, more than body or looks. That aura of confidence contributes to the third area of focus for your mindset, vitality.

> **The first rule is to have vision for your life. The second is to believe in your ability to figure things out. The third is to have fun making your dreams happen no matter how hard it gets. The fourth is to be patient but always persistent. The fifth is to respect and love other people who are also playing the same game of life.**

Vitality

When I was talking about energy, I was also touching on vitality. Vitality isn't something defined by fitness, weight, or strength. It's about having enormous energy levels and just feeling great. It's not just physical. Oozing an aura of vitality comes from being in love with the life you live.

I often meet people who have not exercised for ten years or more. Even after a couple of weeks of exercise someone comments on how much more focused and positive they feel. You can gain focus and positivity immediately by setting a vision for your life and taking steps to improve your physical fitness.

Around 95% of the people who I met in my time as a Health and Lifestyle Coach had a goal to lose weight. Now, I care about weight loss, but it needs to be a side effect of the process. What's more important is how weight loss makes a person feel. What's the emotion a person feels when they get to their target weight? When you dig into the reason behind weight loss, usually it comes down to something like being able to wear a bikini at the beach or to play with your kids. When you probe further, it will often come down to core values and emotions, such as happiness, confidence, and fulfilment.

A massive issue in our society is brain fog. This has a large negative impact on vitality. It's hard to feel energetic when you can't think clearly. One theory of brain fog relates to our diet, and the food that's available to us in supermarkets. When you look at a graph of sugar consumption between the 1700s and the modern world, you'll notice something. In the 1700s, the average person consumed around 1kg of sugar per year. In the 1800s, it was around 20kg per year, in the 1900s

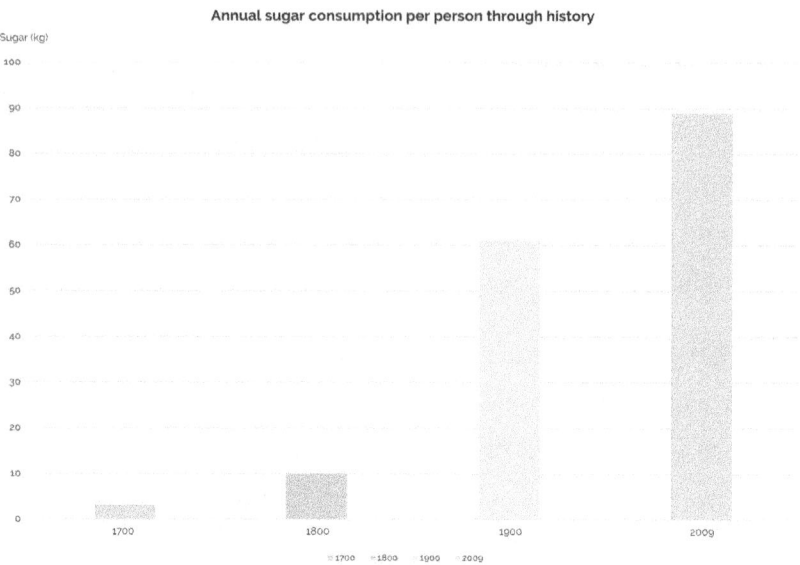

Ironically, before moving into fitness in the mid-nineties, I worked in the head office of a supermarket chain, fielding calls from suppliers wanting to get their products on our shelves. It wasn't great food—full of sugar, salt, and preservatives. The food industry is massive, and the thing to remember is that these massive global suppliers' priority is to look after their bottom line and shareholders. They make more money by selling addictive processed nutrient deficient empty calorie food than by selling something which will fuel your mind and body properly.

Low-quality carbohydrates are foods that usually cause brain fog. Marketing has told us since we were children that breakfast needs to be a carb-rich diet of cereal sweetened with sugar, and we then go off to attack our day. It just doesn't work that way. I can tell you now, I know a few Ironmen, and they don't eat Nutri-Grain.

The top three killers these days are heart disease, cancer, and weight-related diseases. They're all food related. The unnatural toxins used to preserve processed food and make it taste good can cause cancer. Diabetes is out of control, and related to the level of sugar we're consuming.

If you want to increase your vitality, take the simple step of removing processed sugary foods and replacing them with whole meat, fruit, and vegetables. This helps return your body to the type of diet it has evolved to consume.

It's not just food impacting vitality, either. Today we walk ten kilometres less than we did in the 1970s. We live sedentary lives and watch as weight creep adds one kilo a year to our waistlines. You don't notice it from year to year, but after 20 years, you wonder what happened to the thigh gap you had when you were young, or your game of football at school where you could run all game.

You need to burn more calories than you consume. The average person burns 1700 calories, sitting still all day. If you added 300 calories for an exercise session, then reduce your calorie intake to below 2000 calories a day, you should lose weight. When you think that a single meal at McDonald's can easily blow your daily calorie allowance, you can see how these simple changes can make a substantial difference.

Why is vitality so important to a flourishing life? Have you ever overeaten, then wanted to jump up and go for a run? No, you usually slump down and have a little nap while your body works overtime to digest the meal. Food hasn't given you vitality here, it's done the opposite. It's hard to feel positive if you're not feeling physically amazing. If you're feeling sluggish, it impacts your emotional state.

Most people find it's not achieving the end goal of weight loss that makes them feel amazing, but the journey itself. As you take steps to align your physical self with your values and vision, you create momentum in other areas of your life. Minor victories like lifting a weight 5kg more than last week or losing 1kg this week create a sense of achievement. It becomes a ripple effect that spreads throughout your life.

There was one guy I worked with 20 years ago called Mark. He was 143 kilos when I met him. He was 24, an accountant, and never had a girlfriend. You can imagine that he wasn't feeling great about himself. We worked together for 18 months on a journey of losing 50 kilos. He got his weight down to 93 kilos and felt amazing. Everything changed in his life. He left his accounting job during his weight loss journey and became a personal trainer to help people through similar situations. One day, he got set up on a date, and the rest was history. He is now married with three kids, exercises daily, and he's a successful business mentor.

Mark wanted to live life in line with his values but was being held back by his lack of vitality. Weight loss was the catalyst for that journey of change. It will be a unique journey for you. Perhaps it will take a career or relationship change. Maybe it's a change you've never considered.

> **Whatever you are not changing
> you are not choosing.**
>
> **Read that again.**

Imagine what your life would look like, knowing and living in line with your values, having a vision for the future, and elevated levels of energy and vitality. You can see why these three points work together to form the foundation of your mindset. They interact with each other and form the basis of your journey towards flourishing.

Scott Capelin

Step Two: Gratitude, Growth, and Goals

Scott Capelin

Having discovered our values, developed a vision of our life, and defined what vitality looks like for ourselves, we now need to take steps towards bringing those values into reality. We do this by developing an attitude of gratitude, adopting a growth mindset, and setting goals that align with our vision.

Gratitude

Over the years I have noticed that most people could benefit from cultivating a default attitude of gratitude. It's not that people are ungrateful, but people often struggle to see how good we have it. Many of us live in a safe country and can do whatever we want to do. We have a roof over our heads and a bit of money in the bank, making us wealthier than 95% of the world. People do not even realise when they are being negative. Watch what happens when you ask someone how they are, early in the morning, and they say "tired." Or when you ask someone how they have been, and they say "busy." Completely uninspiring answers. Who wants to define themselves as being tired or busy?

> **If you only say one prayer in a day, make it thank you.**
>
> -Rumi

Gratitude can help us when times are tough. We need to train ourselves to look for the gift in every situation. It's tough getting out of bed early in the morning to train, but flip it around to look for the gift in that moment. How fortunate we are to have a comfortable bed with a partner who cares for us. Don't focus on the fact that your bum is a bit bigger and softer than you would like it to be—appreciate the fact that your arms and legs work, and you actually can exercise! We all know of someone who doesn't have this luxury. Gratitude resets our minds. It changes our focus from a negative mindset into a positive one.

Focusing on negativity only draws more negativity. Focusing on what's missing only attracts more of what's missing. Focusing on unhappiness won't bring happiness. When we focus on the negative, we're out of alignment with our values. The fastest way to get where we want is to focus positively on where you are. Focusing on gratitude brings more of what you're grateful for. It gets you ready and makes you hungry for more.

> Gratitude is the healthiest of all human emotions.
>
> The more you express gratitude for what you have, the more likely you will have even more to express gratitude for.
>
> -Zig Ziglar

For many years I've worked closely with a lovely 80-year-old Chinese lady. She looks at the world with a childlike wonder that's absolutely inspiring! It makes the people around her want to see the world as she does. She is so grateful for everything around her. You only need to turn on the news to see money doesn't make people happy. Celebrity couples with everything breaking up or struggling with drugs and alcohol. Focusing on these little things that we can be grateful for helps affect our outlook on life. And while we are talking about the news, do you ever wonder why we need to know about stabbings, traffic jams, wars, and to be hammered with information telling us how bad the economy is? It's so you remain scared and conservative, and don't rock the boat and attack life. The government needs compliant tax payers. Don't watch, read, or listen to the news. Ever. You will not miss anything. Don't let that rubbish fill your mind. It's so sad we think it's normal. Why isn't there any good news? Who controls the news?

No one wants to be an energy vampire, but we all know someone around us who has an aura of negativity. This can dampen our energy when we're in their presence. Gratitude is an energy state. It is uplifting and gives you energy and makes you attractive. If there's only one prayer you ever say, make it 'thank you.'

> **Acknowledging the good that you already have in your life is the foundation for all abundance.**
>
> -Eckhart Tolle

Growth

Every living thing grows. Whether it's a virus, tree, or animal. Every living thing needs to grow to survive. If we are not growing, then we are dying. Think about it. It's one of the six basic human needs to grow. This can be why people who get stuck for a while in life get restless and feel an urge to grow again.

SIX HUMAN NEEDS:
- Certainty
- Variety
- Significance
- Love/Connection
- Growth
- Contribution

As humans, we get into our comfort zone and stay there. It's comfortable! It's nice in there. That can be a problem, as growth often includes pain. When we want to grow a muscle, we first need to cause it pain through weight or resistance training. Only then will it grow stronger and be able to manage more stress. Often, we will stay in a job or relationship we aren't happy with because it provides security and comfort. As humans, we seek to avoid pain, even though growth will mean less pain in the longer term.

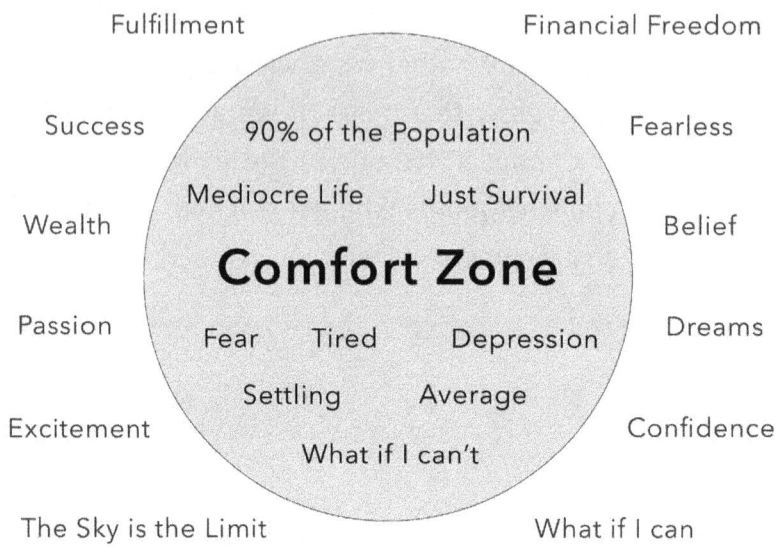

Growth comes from the decisions we make, the people we associate with, and the information we take on board. If we feed negativity into our minds, we grow weeds instead, which can come out in negative habits or behaviours.

> Your mind is a garden
> Your thoughts are the seeds
> You can grow flowers
> Or
> You can grow weeds
>
> - Ritu Ghatourey

The opposite of a growth mindset is a fixed mindset. The fixed mindset says this is my job, I can't change this. A fixed mindset would view redundancy as a setback, while a growth mindset sees it as an opportunity. I can always get another job; I can even start a business. How your mindset plays out in your life is your decision, your choice. Your mindset determines how you grow.

Growth Mindset
Is freedom.

Persevere in the face of failures.
Effort is required to build new skills.
Find inspiration in others success.
Embrace challanges.
Accept criticism.
Desire to learn.
Build abilities.

Fixed Mindset
Is limiting.

Avoid challanges. Give up easily.
Threatened by others success.
Desire to look smart.
Effort is fruitless.
Ignore feedback.
Fixed abilities.

To develop a growth mindset, it's all about how you feed your mind. That's why we started with gratitude in this chapter. An attitude of gratitude goes a long way to cultivating a growth mindset. It's quite important in cultivating gratitude to be careful of what we consume. For example if we spend too much time talking about our problems or gossiping with friends it makes it harder to be grateful and positive in life. You can build upon a positive mindset by reading inspiring books and stories, discovering new and better ways of doing things. You can read or listen to books on personal development, and learn from people who have overcome difficulties in life. There are no losers in life, only learners.

Most people do not realize that as they continue to find things to complain about, they disallow their own physical well-being. Many do not realize that before they were complaining about an aching body or a chronic disease, they were complaining about many other things first. It does not matter if the object of your complaint is about someone you are angry with, behavior in others that you believe is wrong, or something wrong with your own physical body. Complaining is complaining, and it disallows improvement.

-Abraham Hicks

Finally, you make progress by making decisions in line with your values and vision. Most of us live 90-95% of our lives in 1-2 postcodes. It's a huge world out there. Growth leads to confidence and fulfilment.

One of the greatest limitations to growth in our life is ourselves. Everyone has some level of limiting beliefs that stop us from growing beyond a certain point. It might be a belief you can't earn more than $100,000 per year, or can't run more than 5km. Decades ago, people believed you couldn't run a mile in less than four minutes. Until someone did. Then people left, right, and centre started running faster than the 4-minute mile.

We all have our nice cosy comfort zone filled with our limiting beliefs. Often, the fulfilment we seek is on the other side of fear of the unknown, and we need to step up to get through the scary stuff. Remember, courage isn't the absence of fear, it's acknowledging fear and acting anyway.

I used to coach and play a lot of baseball, and everyone wanted to hit a home run. It's a bit like that with life. We may think, if only we can get XYZ, we will be happy in life. In this analogy, everyone thinks they are the batter in a baseball game, trying to hit a home run. But we are not the batter, we are the pitcher, throwing the ball, and the universe is batting. The more times we throw the ball, the more likely the universe can hit us at a home run. You can always do the bare minimum with anything in life, or you can choose to be more, to grow more. To be a better parent or spouse. To upskill at your job or volunteer to contribute to others. You can always grow! All you have to do is keep throwing pitches and the universe will decide which one to hit for a home run when the time is right

Goals

We've done a lot of work on our mindset. Now we need to take steps towards who we want to be. We can't just get up and go. We need to have a plan and to do that; we need to set goals for ourselves.

Goals are important when we want to create the life we want. It's like a trip to the supermarket. If we prepare a list and keep referring to it while we're shopping, we can usually get through the shopping faster, on budget, and with the things we want. Without having that list, we wander through the supermarket, continually remembering or forgetting the things we are there to buy and buying a whole heap of things we don't need.

You have the opportunity when creating goals to create your perfect day. What would make your diet a ten out of ten and still be enjoyable? Can you come up with 3 tasty, healthy meals that could form the basis of your nutrition plan? What activities will make your day fulfilling? Most people don't reach the end of their life and wish they'd worked harder. They wished they filled their life with things that truly mattered to them. For me, I include things like speaking to my parents, travelling with my family, hugging my kids, and helping others on their journey through life. These things result in deep fulfilment for me and are perfectly in line with my values.

When you have your list of goals, it narrows your focus and brings awareness each day to the things you want to work towards. It reminds you of what you truly value in life. It's important to realise we can set a goal we want to achieve, and still fail. What's worse, though? Setting a goal you want to achieve, and falling short? Or not setting a goal in life and failing at something you didn't want to do?

You may as well have a go at what's important to you.

We get so caught up in life. We constantly lose focus the moment a crisis presents itself or we get distracted. Goals help us refocus, keep us heading in the direction we want to have.

If you're anything like me at the beginning of my journey, I hated the word discipline. It sounded like I was going to deprive myself or lose my freedom. But what I learned further along this journey is that discipline equals freedom. When you have the discipline to make decisions that align with your values and your vision, it creates the life you want. It eliminates distraction, saves time, and keeps you on the road to happiness.

How do you create a goal?

The first step is to start with a simple template. Setting out the principal areas of my life and the values I have for each area. Then I break down those areas into what I want to achieve in 3 months, 12 months, and 3 years.

The 3-month timeframe is great because it's short. It keeps your focus sharp. You need to ensure that the goal is achievable because it's not far away. Make it small but inspiring.

The 12-month timeframe is interesting because we often overestimate what we can achieve in a year. Again, you need to make these achievable, but representing a big step towards your vision statement. The 12-month goal can be incredibly powerful, as we can plan how to make the next year the best year yet. This timeframe doesn't need to be big goals either to make a difference. Imagine how much difference to your relationship a date night each week would make. Or your sense of enjoyment of life to book a holiday twice in the next 12 months in advance.

Meanwhile, the 3-year goal is the fun one. It's usually where you have a big, hairy, audacious goal (BHAG). That's where you might set your goal of a change of career or running your own business. Often these are the goals that tie strongly in with your vision for your life. Sometimes those big goals could take much longer, even 10 years and longer, but these represent steps towards that life you desire.

Mostly when we think about goals, what we're usually thinking about is something like, I want to lose 5 kilos. But that by itself is not particularly inspiring. Goals need to be inspiring. They need to get you out of bed when it's cold to put in the effort to create your vision. You want your goals and your life vision to be so compelling that you jump out of bed in the morning and feel empowered through the day!

Which goal is more inspiring for you? To lose 5 kilos or to look great in a bikini at the holiday you have planned in three months? Is it more inspiring to say you want to get fit or to complete the City to Surf in three months? Whatever your goal is, it needs to be of value to you. You want to refer to your values and your vision statement constantly when setting them.

Goals also need to be achievable. You need to complete them within the timeframe you've set. Part of setting goals is achieving wins towards your ideal life. There is immense satisfaction to be found in achieving a goal towards which you've been working.

You won't achieve all your goals, and that's alright. Even myself, I'm a driven guy and I estimate that I've only achieved around 40% of my goals in the last couple of decades. The important thing is that I've achieved heaps more on the journey that I never set out to achieve.

Sometimes I prefer to use the word "intentions" when talking about goals because as long as I'm focused on my values, I may not achieve my goals but achieve something better along the way.

Finally, once we've set our goals, we need to surrender them. Let go of our control of them. It's a way of thinking that takes the weight of those goals off our shoulders. It's a way of being open to everything and nothing. We'll talk more about surrender in step five.

Step Three: Passion, Purpose, and Positivity

Scott Capelin

So far, we have identified our values, clarified our vision, and understood what it takes to live with vitality; we have cultivated an attitude of gratitude and a growth mindset, and set ourselves inspiring goals. What's next?

Now we come to living a life full of passion, positivity and living with purpose. These areas are all linked because a life without these three things can be bland and empty. These are the spices that make life exciting!

Passion

Imagine dragging yourself through a day where you're doing things you don't enjoy. It would be a day void of any form of passion, and hard work just to get up in the morning. Time drags out moment by moment. You might even feel like one of those wind-up toys set loose and you get to the end of the day and have no more to give, and then have to wind yourself up for the next day.

Sadly, this scenario is many people's reality. Now compare that to a life of passion. Imagine waking up in the morning excited to go about your day! Excited about what you can achieve! Full of energy to get stuck into whatever you do. Time flies, and it feels like that passion is pulling you along almost effortlessly! There are still rough days, but you have this deep sense of passion, along with your vision, which means you can get through anything.

> **He who has a strong enough why can bear almost any how.**
>
> -Friedrich Nietzche

Passion ties in closely with your values. The more aligned your life is with your values, the more passionate you feel about your life. You're pursuing what you truly value in life. You have consciously prioritised the things that are most important to you, and the result is a life you are deeply passionate about.

The opposite is also true about whenever you feel unhappy. It's likely because you're not living in line with your values. It's a signal that something's not right. Something needs to change. An example is having a job that doesn't fulfil you. It can get you down, you might turn to alcohol or bad foods to fill the void or buy things you don't need that result in temporary happiness. Then you go back to work day after day, week after week, creating a cycle that can quickly become passionless.

Now, if you have a value of family and what you're working for is to put food on the table, pay off a mortgage, and put your children through school, then that cycle has a purpose that can contribute to your sense of passion. But if it's a job you don't enjoy, then only one of your values doesn't align, and it drags you down. If your value in this example is family, then the job you don't like may be a means to an end. But if you come home cranky, and stay in a job you don't like for the long term, what kind of example is this setting for your kids (your greatest value)? Would you want them to do the same when they become adults? What kind of role model are you?

Maybe living with passion is something you've felt is hard to find, some dreamland of fairies and rainbows, the realm of rich people with unlimited resources. The reality of living with passion is taking small steps in line with our values. As we take those small steps pursuing our passion, step by step, it takes over our life.

> **It's the possibility of having a dream come true that makes life interesting.**
>
> -Paulo Coelho, The Alchemist

How can we take that cycle that's partially aligned with your values and connect it with passion? Let's face it, you wouldn't be working at all if it didn't align with one of your values. Maybe you need to align your non-work time with a different value or hobby. Maybe you need to align yourself in your job to engage in what you're passionate about the job again (even if it means taking a pay cut).

And maybe the step you need to take is create a BHAG and back yourself into something which you'll be truly passionate about. It all starts with knowing your values.

Purpose

It's hard to talk about passion without talking about having a sense of purpose in life. They are related, but each has a different role to play. You can feel passion through pursuing a hobby or loving your spouse, but a sense of purpose gets you up in the morning. Purpose pushes you through challenges, and purpose leads to fulfilment and meaning.

Many people feel invisible. They feel like their presence on the planet doesn't matter. They feel like they don't have a purpose. One of the greatest questions of life is "why am I here?"

> **Money, like health, love, happiness, and all forms of miraculous happenings that you want to create for yourself, is the result of your living purposefully. It is not a goal unto itself.**
>
> - Dr. Wayne Dyer

Where do you draw purpose from in your life? Many draw it from their job or role, throwing 70 hours a week into a corporate career, earning good money, feeling important. For some people it comes from being a parent, or helping others in some way.

Purpose gives you a sense of confidence and significance (another of the six human needs). These are both particularly important to our sense of self-esteem. You want to feel you matter. You want to feel you're contributing positively to your community.

Once again, knowing your values is a vital component to discovering purpose, since it will align with those, but even greater than that that it's linked to your vision. Your vision will encompass your purpose in life. Purpose powers vitality and pushes you to grow. It becomes the powerhouse of your life.

What gives you the biggest sense of purpose in your life?

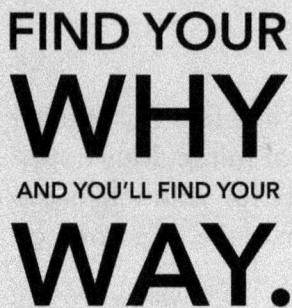

- John C. Maxwell

Positivity

You may think that we already covered positivity when we talked about gratitude in the last chapter. Positivity grows out of gratitude. It's hard to be positive if we aren't thankful for what we already have. The more we are grateful, the more positive we are. Gratitude and positivity become attractors in our lives. This means that the more positive and grateful we are on a regular basis, the more good things we will attract to us.

> **Every time you praise something, every time you appreciate something, every time you feel good about something, you are telling the Universe, "More of this, please."**
>
> -Abraham Hicks

Earlier, we talked about energy vampires. They are people who suck the energy out of those around them. A person filled with positivity builds up the people around them and seeks to cultivate gratitude in the lives of others. Positive people naturally attract other positive people who all work to grow together. Your vibe attracts your tribe. It's more than just being grateful. It's an attitude you choose to have. It's more about the person you are. It's about finding the gift in every situation rather than the downside. Are you the kind of person other people want to be around?

> We are all flesh and bones. We all come from the same universal source. However, the ones who do more than just exist, the ones who fan the flames of their human potential and truly savor the magical dance of life do different things than those whose lives are ordinary. Foremost among the things that they do is adopt a positive paradigm about their world and all that is in it.
>
> - Robin Sharma

Life is going to be full of challenges. We all know this. Being a positive person is knowing that setbacks will happen, however they aren't permanent or defining. Life is about how you react to it. When facing a challenge in life, you could jump straight onto the negative bandwagon, or you could react with faith that life will work out. Everything happens for a reason. The difficult part of having faith when you are going through a hard patch is that at the time you don't know the reason! Have faith in the bigger picture.

It's not always easy. If you're out of a job and having a hard time finding one, can you stay positive in the light of that? If you're going through a chronic illness in yourself or a loved one, there are going to be days of despair.

A negative person might respond with, "I've always had bad luck, I always get the red lights, good things never happen to me, I knew that would not work out, I will always be overweight!" That negativity then attracts those things, and the negative person says, "see, I was right!"

A positive person is the opposite. They might respond with, "Things are getting better every day, I believe I can do this, support is available to me, I'm a good person, I am worthy of love, happiness, success, and fulfilment."

To cultivate a positive mindset, the first step is to always look for the positive in every situation. Let's take a simple one like rain. Many people struggle to see the gift of rain at the moment it's pouring down. However, rain means food and water, rain has a peaceful sound, rain means cooler weather, greener grass. Rain is a gift for everyone. It brings life.

Finally, be playful! It can help to not take things too seriously. Worry less. If it isn't going to matter in five years, don't worry about it for 5 minutes.

Scott Capelin

Step Four: Conviction, Connection, and Contribution

Having worked through passion, positivity, and purpose, we now need to add a layer to the life we are creating. In this chapter, we will build our conviction, deepen our connections, and ultimately, contribute to our community and the world on a larger scale.

Conviction

I wanted to start with conviction in this chapter, as it leads straight out of purpose. When we have a purpose, conviction naturally follows. Conviction is the definite knowledge that you are doing something worthwhile, and that you are on the right path. It gives you confidence. It enables you to break free of the shackles of society's confines and ignore the opinions and thoughts of others. Conviction is the deep knowledge that you are doing what's best for you and others, and this type of certainty increases your self-esteem. When people with small minds question your decision, conviction keeps you on your true path.

There's one woman I've worked with who went from being an employee to opening her own business. This can be a hard journey for the best of us, and she did it successfully. What happened during the journey was that those around her were upset about her success. Firstly, they told her not to open her own business. They thought she should stay as an employee like them. Her desire to live a richer life highlighted their inadequacies, and they responded by attempting to tear her down. They told her not to open a business, and they pointed out the things that could go wrong. However, her conviction made her ignore the negative comments from her family and friends and kept on her track. She went on to achieve immense success. She had tough times, but she prevailed.

How do you become the person you want to be? One of the six basic human needs we all have is certainty, and conviction feeds deeply into that need. It gives you a foundation to work with as you make each decision towards your vision and your goals, helping you stay laser focused.

Conviction isn't something you can simply manufacture. You grow it in your life by living in line with your values and vision. Each time you decide to align with those, it will reinforce your conviction and create a momentum that can become unstoppable (especially when combined with positivity).

Connection

Connection can be hard to define. On one level, it can refer to our connection with each other, people forming a community, which is incredibly important. Often, people who feel disconnected from their community will become lonely. You can be connected to your work if the nature of your work aligns with your intrinsic values. You can have a deep, intimate emotional connection with your intimate partner. See how powerful the right connections are? And imagine you don't like your work and your relationship is going nowhere—see how soul destroying a lack of connection can be?

In this book, I want to go deeper and talk about the connection to yourself. We've already talked about living in alignment with our values. The ultimate connection we can attain is the spiritual connection we gain by living in line with our values. Connecting with who we are, and living our lives in line with our values, deepens that connection to ourselves and the universe. This inner connection generates passion and purpose, and it only happens when we are true to ourselves.

From this spiritual inner connection grows a connection with others. Have you ever been around someone who is genuinely comfortable with who they are? They are nice to be around, and often you can't explain why. They already seem to live their best life, brimming with positivity, and you just want to spend time with them because they make you feel better. Anthony Robbins says that when you see someone you think is sexy, it's not their looks that are creating the attractive aura. It's their freedom. When someone is free it's a very alluring quality.

How do your daily choices build your connection with others? Some studies say your choice of a life partner is responsible for up to 90% of your life's happiness, but what about your choices in cultivating your connection with them? This mindset journey we have been working through gets enhanced when connected with your partner, who is on a similar journey. You're able to share your values and your vision and become accountable to each other on the journey. Marriages come unstuck when partners don't grow together, or they don't grow at all, or if one person grows and one person doesn't, or if two people grow in different directions. And there is a pretty huge chance of one of these scenarios unfolding during a 40-year marriage!

Connection is also linked to community. Most people have a home and work in their lives, but we all need a third place where we feel a deep-seated sense of connection. As human beings, we have a deep desire to feel a part of something, and feel like we are progressing somewhere. This is where growth becomes about more than just yourself; it becomes about those around you.

You can find this sense of community in many places. Whether that's school, with friends, a community group, the gym, or your sporting group. It's a place where we feel connected with like-minded people and can create a feeling of fulfilment.

Finally, connection also manifests in connectedness to something greater than ourselves. For some, this is religion. For others, it's a connection to the universe, a charitable organisation, or a greater cause that draws us to contribute to others. Whatever your values are, the connection comes about by living aligned with those values.

Contribution

Contribution is a massive thing for many people. Again, it's one of the six human needs. Often, it helps us feel worthy as human beings in that we aren't just looking after ourselves, we're helping people around us. That outward focus helps grow positivity in yourself and usually grows out of having a purpose. Helping others makes us feel good about ourselves. It's one of those activities in life where in giving you receive back more than you give yourself. Being a parent can be the ultimate act of contribution. Contribution results in fulfilment. Some people say that the purpose of life is to serve others – not just look after ourselves.

This desire to help others is simply part of who we are. Think about that for a moment. It's not just a good thing to do. It can be a shortcut to living a fulfilling life aligned with your values. I used to believe that your level of happiness, life satisfaction, and even your income is all linked to the amount of value you are adding to the world. I suppose I still do think that. If you aren't happy—ask yourself if you are helping anyone. There are three things we can give to others, which are our time, our knowledge, and our money. And that is the order of importance.

Connectedness and contribution link closely. It's difficult to contribute if you're not first connected on some level of your life. However, the contribution can also be a way to cultivate connectedness. Volunteering for a cause you believe in can be the fastest way to plant yourself in a community of like-minded people with similar values. The wonderful thing is, the more you contribute as part of a community, the faster connection builds with that community.

Living with a philosophy of contribution is about having an attitude toward serving others. It looks for ways to serve. It sees contribution as a responsibility.

Each of us has unique skills we can use to help others. Accountants can contribute as treasurers for charities, handymen can help build houses for the homeless, business owners can help run charity projects efficiently. Whatever your skills, there are a vast number of ways to contribute once you look.

I mentioned earlier that contribution is a shortcut for living aligned with your values, but it's important to find a cause you're passionate about that fits with your purpose. Otherwise, a contribution can become a drain on your vitality rather than empowering it.

There are so many charities and causes out there you can help, and the best way you can help one is through engaging with who you are. Contributing financially to a cause that you believe in is a simple way to engage with contribution, but the most fulfilling is when you contribute directly. For example, in running health clubs, one way I contribute is when I come across someone who needs what I provide and genuinely can't afford it, I'll give them a free membership. Easy for me to do and it has a significant impact on the person. They may ask how they can repay the favour and I'll ask them to pay it forward. Perhaps there's a way they can help someone using their resources and skills? Watching them change their lives and become empowered is extremely rewarding.

Contribution can be on a small level too. My elderly father lives next door to a lovely Indian couple who often make him dinner. That's how they contribute. And my father mows their lawn. It all goes hand in hand. What goes around usually comes around.

Can you see how each of these aspects of mindset is reinforcing each other? Growing a flourishing mindset is a bit like cultivating a garden. Values and vision feed everything in our mindset, leading us to set goals feeding our passion. Gratitude feeds positivity, which combined with purpose and passion, feeds our conviction. Vitality and growth, combined with purpose, drive connection and contribution.

Each step of cultivating this mindset supports another, growing the garden of your mind, growing, and feeding each other into a life that can flourish into the level of fulfilment you have dreamed of.

Scott Capelin

Step Five: Strength, Self-Image, and Surrender

Scott Capelin

As we continue to cultivate our mindset, we come to the areas of mental strength, developing a healthy self-image, and the concept of surrendering ourselves to the journey.

Strength

Some of the strongest people in the world aren't those with physical strength. They're the people who have mental resilience in the face of challenges. They're the people who have overcome setbacks and go on to live a successful life with a happy disposition, never looking back, and focusing on the great thing about their life, and not on their problems or what they have lost, or what could have been. They understand challenges happen and they bounce back stronger than ever. They are not celebrities or super heroes – they are everyday people getting through life.

When I talk about strength, there are two types I talk about. The first is strength when you don't have a choice. If a family member dies without warning, suddenly you have no choice but to be strong for the sake of the family and friends around you. Someone needs to step up and look after them, take care of the funeral arrangements, to support the grieving process. This requires you to be strong, and quite often you may discover strength you didn't know you had. Same situation if a business fails, or if your partner leaves you. You have to keep moving forward.

Then there's the strength you require when you DO have a choice. An example is if you have a job that you hate but it pays the bills, or if you are in a relationship that is not fulfilling. This is when real strength is required. You are not forced into change, and you have to make a conscious, hard decision. Quite often people do not make the hard decision to leave the job or the relationship because, well, it's hard! So, what happens then? Five years later that person could be in the same crappy job, or the same troubled relationship, and be even more miserable. The bottom line is that if you don't make the difficult decision, you are not strong. This ties into our earlier discussion about certainty. Even though the job and the relationship in this example is bad, people will remain in these undesirable situations because leaving has a large amount of uncertainty, so they would rather stay with the certainty they know. The job pays the bills. It is easier to stay in an unfulfilling relationship than to leave, find somewhere else to live, sort out the finances, and decide who keeps the dog.

> **When you want something, all the universe conspires in helping you to achieve it.**
>
> -Paulo Coelho, The Alchemist

To promote strength in your mindset, you need to have a powerful element of conviction and a positive self-image. Conviction is necessary to make the hard choices. Meanwhile, you need to have a strong self-image that says you are worthy of positive change and, by making that change, you're going to come out in a better place. You can see how Faith plays a key role here too. The unknown is scary.

Strength also flows from a life lived in line with your values and vision. The closer you live to those, the firmer your conviction, and the more mental resilience you'll have in the face of challenges. Life is distracting, and without mental strength, it can take you off your path so easily and back into a life of comfort. And despite being comfortable, there is nothing good about the comfort zone.

Surrender

Surrender is one area of mindset that can be hard to understand, and that's alright, because it can be confusing. Having been through the journey of discovering our values, writing our vision, setting goals, activating our passion, and finding a sense of purpose, we feel like we have carved a non-negotiable path to our best life. We want to take steps right now to make it happen. However, you need to surrender in order to bring your dreams to fruition.

> **Have a mind that is open to everything and attached to nothing.**
>
> - Dr. Wayne Dyer

Surrender isn't about giving up or not caring. It's knowing some things will go our way and others won't, and there's a reason for the things that don't, and that's ok. Sometimes you can have a dream and put so much focus and energy into it and it still fails. Surrender is about letting go and letting it happen. It's about relaxing into the flow of life. Trusting the universe will work everything out. It's about reducing stress and anxiety about things we can't control. It is about knowing that everything happens for a reason, and that everything will be okay in the end, and if it's not okay, it's not the end!

We all know that one person looking for a relationship. They're desperate to make it happen and are white knuckling their way through date after date, hoping this next person is the right one. The problem is that desperation pushes people away.

If a person sets their vision on finding a partner, they can focus their attention and energy on making themselves the best person they can be by living in line with their values. They can suddenly become incredibly attractive to a potential suitor.

The same goes for business. We can walk into a sales presentation desperate for a sale, and put our potential client off. However if we walk into the meeting genuinely believing that we have the best solution for their problems, we find they will gravitate to us and want to work together.

I've been through that journey myself, pouring energy and focus into a business, and it didn't work out the way I hoped it would. I didn't have all the information then, though. I didn't know how it would end up.

Now I've ended up in another business. It is the most fulfilling business of my life. I collaborate with wonderful people and have businesses that create more freedom which allows me to travel and spend more time with my family (my highest values) than ever before. It wouldn't have been possible without leaving the previous business. Everything happens for a reason. Life is full of ups and downs. It's not about what happens, but how we react.

Part of surrender is loving yourself just the way you are. It's accepting that you are worthy of good things and knowing that you deserve to attract them. If what we do is always blame others and make excuses for bad things that happen to us, then we are telling ourselves we have no control over what happens. When we take ownership and responsibility, it becomes liberating. Why bother wasting energy on things we can't control?

Surrender any attachment how other people think and react, you can't change that. Surrender control over external events, like the weather, elections, or a pandemic, you can't control them. Focus on the things you can control, like your mindset, your decisions, and your attitude. One of my most fundamental secrets to inner peace is the knowledge that I cannot control what anyone else says, does, or thinks, so I never try to, and it's a very peaceful feeling. Similarly, nobody else can ever understand the reasons for your goals, desires, and wants, so don't bother explaining it to them. Everyone has different values, and people look at the world through the filter or lens of their own values, so how can we all possibly be in agreement with anything?

I want to add a short paragraph on a big topic here. Earlier I mentioned that I have set lots of goals in life and not achieved some of them. I put in the effort, and things didn't work out the way I wanted them to. There is something called "Resistance" which is the ultimate goal blocker. What is resistance? It comes in many forms, and it's mainly mental and emotional, and it's all about the energy you are taking on board and giving out, and it's all about your thoughts. Examples are:

- Saying to yourself that you aren't sure you can do it
- Wondering how you will do it
- Reading negative news articles about finance and the economy
- All the ugly emotions such as jealousy, greed, anger, and revenge
- Negative self-talk
- Not believing in yourself

> ### Florence Scovel Shinn said in 1925
>
> "Nothing on Earth can resist an absolutely non-resistant person." To be in a non-resistant state means that everything you desire is magnetized to you immediately.
>
> ### How does it feel to be non-resistant?
>
> Well, when you are resistant you feel heavy. When you are non-resistant you feel light. It is similar to floating on water you must be non-resistant to be able to float. It is a feeling of calmness, total relaxation, and letting go of all tension. As you surrender to this state of effortlessness, the water will completely support you. That is the feeling of non-resistance. When you are in that place you are an irresistible magnet, and the Universe will support you completely.

Society conditions us to think we have to work hard to get anything worthwhile in life. In some ways, that's true. You must act. You can jump into the river and start swimming. But you can swim upstream against the current, or you can gain more momentum by swimming downstream. Whether you believe in a higher force guiding us, the universe, or just in our ability to make the best of any situation, surrender is often key to bringing your vision into reality.

Self-Image

We are often our own worst critics. Have you ever stopped to examine some things we said to ourselves? If we were our own best friends, and other people heard what we said to ourselves, they'd be telling us to ditch them.

Self-image is more than just self-esteem. It's about how we see ourselves as a person. Do you want to see yourself as someone worthy of happiness, success, fulfilment, and love? Or do you want to accept an image of yourself that's mediocre?

> **To fall in love with yourself is the first secret to happiness**
>
> -Robert Morley

A person with poor self-image stays in a terrible job or relationship when they know they should get out. This is not because they can't do better, but because they think they can't do better. Maybe you'd eat a packet of chocolate biscuits every night because it makes you feel better. It's comforting, but you don't think you'll ever have great health, so it doesn't matter if you eat healthily.

A positive self-image says you deserve good things in life. That you can make choices to better your life and grow into a better person. You can make choices at work, in relationships, and in health to give you the life you deserve.

In a physical sense, sometimes our body doesn't look the way we want it to. Rather than saying "I don't like my legs," stop and appreciate your legs because they allow you to walk anywhere you want to go, and because they are strong, and they are part of your healthy body.

The key to growing a healthy self-image is to start feeling good about yourself, right where you are now. This is where passion, purpose, and a growth mindset all feed into transforming your self-image. Making those small decisions through the strength of your conviction that aligns with your values and your vision immerses yourself in things that improve your self-image. Contributing to a community where you are connected speeds it up. Practising Gratitude and developing Positivity creates an optimistic point of view where you just walk taller feeling better about yourself.

Step Six: Faith, Fulfilment, and Focus

Scott Capelin

Can you see how all these different aspects of mindset all work together to create a rich and prosperous life? In this chapter, we're going to continue to grow our flourishing life with deep faith, a powerful level of fulfilment that adds joy to life, and a laser-sharp focus.

Faith

When most people think of faith, they're thinking about religion, but it's much more than that. When I'm talking about faith, I am talking about faith in yourself, and faith that everything in your life will constantly get better. Faith flows strongly from surrender and self-image. They work hand in hand. It's hard to surrender if you don't have faith that your vision is possible, that you can get there, and that things will improve.

Faith is believing in something you can't see, touch, or feel with your physical senses. Faith asks, what tools do I have within me to manifest the life I desire? Faith tells you that everything will be ok.

Belief is more important than intelligence. If you believe that anything is possible, then it is. If you believe that something is not possible, then it's not. Do you want to play to win, or play just to not lose?

> **Take the first step in faith.
> You don't have to see the whole staircase,
> just take the first step.**
>
> - Martin Luther King

Faith and focus work together. There's a saying that worrying is praying for what you don't want. When you worry about things, you're putting a focused thought out there, and attracting it right back to you. Worrying about something doesn't fix it. Your happiness can't depend on external events because you can't control them. If you can change the thing you're worried about, then fix it. If you can't, then don't worry about it. You're only wasting focus and vitality on something you can't change.

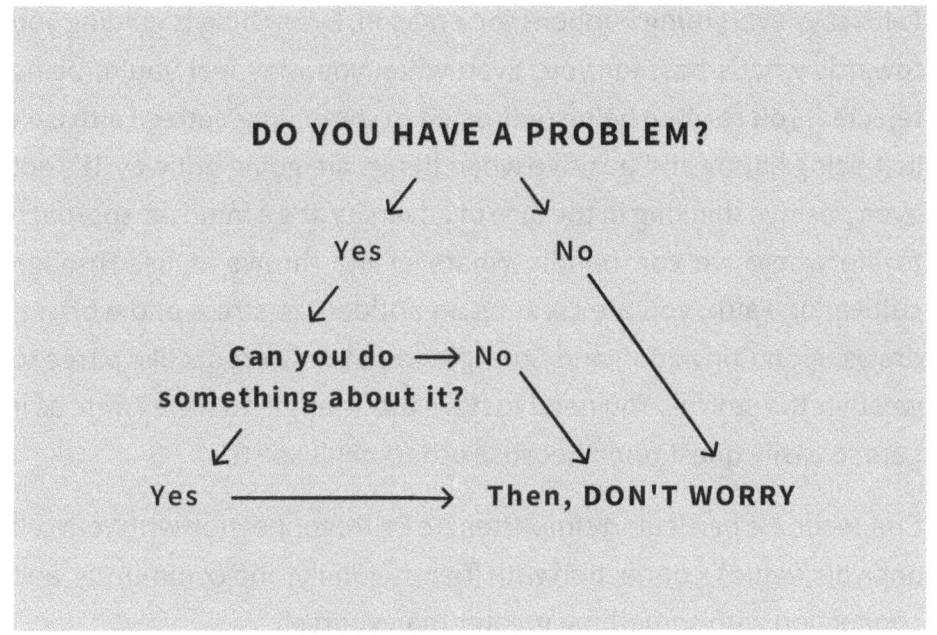

The Law of Attraction dictates that you get what you focus on. If you are thinking about sad things, you will get more of them. If you are thinking about something you don't want to happen, you are actually playing a role in the creation of it happening. If you think about driving a nice car, having loyal friends, and being financially abundant, you are planting the seeds in your subconscious mind for this to happen. You don't need to worry about how it will happen. Just try and feel the feelings of what it is like when this vision is reality. Think from the vision, not towards it. Imagine yourself there. When you plant a mango seed you don't get a rose growing in its place. You get what you plant. Your thoughts are the seed of your future life. Think of everything as energy and know that what you put out is what you get back. That's why there's no point holding a grudge, hating someone, or trying to get revenge. These toxic thoughts only hurt you.

Faith says everything happens for a reason. Everything is guiding you towards what's best for you. Even when you may feel you're being rejected, you're often being redirected to something better. Faith isn't just being happy and positive when things are going our way. It's not even positive thinking in the face of adversity. It's a mindset approach to life where we can handle whatever life throws at us. Through cultivating Faith, you are creating an antidote to stress and worry. It draws upon Conviction and Strength to put down roots like a tree to weather the storms. You need to have the strength to have Faith, as it gets so easily questioned because others can't see it.

Connection is particularly important to Faith, connection with yourself and your values, connection with friends, family, and community, and connection with something greater than yourself.

Follow your heart but take your brain with you.

You may go through a tough patch in life. Maybe it's a period of financial stress or a breakup. Five years down the road, you could be making money a different way and be with the most amazing spouse, but you wouldn't have arrived there without the journey you're walking now.

Faith trusts that every rejection or disappointment is guiding me towards what's best for me. Every time I thought someone rejected me, I was being redirected towards something better. We don't have all the information. I love it when people say no! I just think "Next!"

> **Wisdom is looking back at your life and realising that every single event, person, place and idea was part of the perfected experience you needed to build your dream. Not one was a mistake.**
>
> - John Demartini

Fulfilment

Fulfilment is more than happiness. If I told you a joke, and you laughed, for a moment you're happy. Fulfilment is more of a deep sense of being on the right path. It's the ultimate result of living in line with your values. It's also different from satisfaction. Satisfaction comes from achieving a goal or a win, but Fulfilment goes even deeper than that. Fulfilment results in the creation of a deep positive energy which stems from living the life we're supposed to. When we aren't feeling fulfilled, we feel restless, distracted. When we feel fulfilled, we feel peaceful, yet empowered. A life of passion and purpose leads to a feeling of fulfilment.

The journey you're on to a flourishing life is not about the goals you set. Some you'll achieve and others you won't. That will not give you fulfilment. It's about heading in the right direction.

One woman I worked with wanted to lose 20 kilos and even at the very beginning of her health journey when she was nowhere near the end-goal she felt very fulfilled because she was seeing progress towards the life she wants to create. In fact, many successful people look back and say that the best part of their achievements wasn't the end result, it was the journey along the way. Goals are not always about the end game – they are about the person you become in the process.

> **It's not about the goal. It's about growing to become the person that can accomplish that goal.**
>
> - Tony Robbins

Focus

What is focus? When we look through the lens of a camera, the area in focus is sharp and clear, while the areas out of focus become blurry. It's the same with life. When you've set your goals, you're living with conviction, pursuing your vision, and living with purpose. Focus helps us stay on track.

Life is full of distraction. It's so easy to get distracted along the path to a life of meaning. Faith and Focus work hand in hand to help pull you through the worst times of life. Faith says you can get through, while Focus helps you stay on track through those tough times, working on the things which can make a difference in those times.

We cultivate Focus in our lives by reminding ourselves what our values, vision, and goals are. We go back to the very start of this process. A fantastic way to keep yourself Focused is by reading out your vision statement daily in the morning to remind yourself of the life you want to create, then Focus on your goals throughout the day.

Step Seven: Affirmations, Abundance and Action

Scott Capelin

Describing the steps to a flourishing mindset is almost complete! There's one last element to cover. In this chapter, we look at reinforcing our vision with affirmations, adopting a mindset of abundance, and taking action to bring a stimulating, inspiring life into reality!

Affirmations

Affirmations are the repetition of a positive phrase, a statement of the result we're seeking. It's something simple, like "I am a master of money." Another is "I am a positive person who brings joy everywhere I go," or "I'm a strong leader, an incredible business owner, and an amazing wife and mother." They don't have to be too formal. Repeat them to yourself whenever you remember. It increases your level of positive self-talk. Muhammad Ali used to say, "I am the greatest!" and it worked for him!

You say an affirmation in the first person, in the present tense, as if it's already a reality. Your subconscious doesn't know the difference between the past, the present, and the future. This is why imagination is so powerful.

What you're working to achieve with affirmations is to embed into your subconscious an expectation around your vision. Imagine expecting abundance, believing there's so much out there for you to be, do, and have. Imagine how much easier it would be for the abundance all around you to flow to you. Imagine being able to convince yourself you really can have whatever you want in life.

You design affirmations to help you overcome negativity and fear in your life. Fear is just an emotion not often based on reality. We all have irrational fears we've picked up through life which can hold us back from creating the life we desire.

Affirmations are also more than positive thinking. We spoke earlier in the book about how we develop negative self-image through negative self-talk. Instead of doing damage through that negative self-talk, we are instead choosing to speak positively about ourselves. We are building up positivity and a healthy self-image. Affirmations keep the person you want to be at the front of your conscious mind. We so easily forget who we want to be and relax back into comfortable patterns.

Affirmations are best repeated regularly to reinforce them. A few ways you can do that effectively is to mix up a few different methods. Some people react best to saying them in front of a mirror, others write them out, others record them and listen to them while they sleep. You could do a combination of all of these to engage your subconscious mind more fully.

Affirmations need to be more than just repeating words. You must engage your emotions and your Faith with your affirmations. Empty words will produce empty results. Engaged emotions help you connect with yourself and your greater power.

Our brains work off neural pathway patterns. What we're trying to achieve is to create new pathways through these affirmations. If you hear something enough times, said with enough emotion and meaning, you're going to believe it. These new neural pathways program your brain to override any existing limiting thoughts you have in your mind. Your subconscious mind believes the affirmation is real and universal forces work to bring your desire to fruition in the physical world.

When creating your affirmations, you want to link them closely to your values, vision, goals, and purpose. This is why we've worked through all this already. This step is just taking that work, creating 5-10 short sentences to affirm those things. Don't over complicate it. You could have an affirmation that says:

- Money flows to me freely and easily
- I attract amazing opportunities every week
- I live life with the partner of my dreams
- My partner and I support each other's values and are always there for each other
- I'm an amazing parent
- I take amazing holidays every year!
- I am in amazing health, and I love my body!
- All the help I need is available to me
- I'm always in the right place at the right time to meet the right person to make the right deal

They should mean something to you. It should be fun to write and say. Laminate them and put them in your bathroom mirror, or repeat them while driving in your car as part of your morning routine.

Abundance

Saying an affirmation can be difficult in the middle of a tough situation. There's often a little switch in our brain that says, "that's not true, that's not possible." That's where abundance comes in.

Have you ever stopped to consider that we are living in a world with incredible abundance? There is more food produced than we can eat. We have an abundance of water, shelter, clothing, and wealth. There is no limit to the resources available to us. There are a thousand ways for those resources to come to us.

Imagine being convinced that there's more than enough resources around you to achieve the Vision you've been dreaming of. The opposite of a philosophy of abundance is a mentality of scarcity. That's where you think resources are finite and you don't share, or you think that in order for you to win, someone else has to lose. Imagine the energy that creates? If you think in this limited way you will be putting that energy out into the world and attracting it back to you. It's like the jealous boyfriend that doesn't let his partner go out. Ironically, he is trying to protect his relationship, but the behaviour he displays is pushing his partner away. You can't get to abundance from a place of lack any more than you can get to a place of happiness while you're having thoughts of unhappiness.

Abundance is more than a positive mindset. It's a feeling of acceptance, built on a foundation of faith, in the knowledge that there are so many resources freely available to us all. We can share our resources, helping others. A scarcity mentality may hold on to what we have out of fear, while an abundance mindset says we can use our talents, time, and money them to help others because there's more than enough to go around.

> **A beautiful day begins with a beautiful mindset. When you wake up, take a second to think about what a privilege it is to simply be alive & healthy. The moment we start acting like life is a blessing I assure you it will start to feel like one.**

This isn't limited to physical abundance. I mentioned earlier that all matter is energy. Look at the sun. It has billions of years of fuel left to energise our planet. Love can never run out. Love multiplies when we give it out in abundance. It gets returned with interest. There is abundance all around us and accepting that reality is a huge step towards a flourishing life.

If you are ever feeling down, try and change your state. State is another word for mood. You can change your state by listening to music, exercising, or having a nap!

Action

Nothing happens unless you take action. I've intentionally left this one until last. When you cultivate a flourishing mindset, taking inspired action is natural. It's almost inevitable. You can't help but take steps towards your vision and goals because they're filling your mind and your focus. You can work on your mindset as much as you want, but if you don't take action, you'll get nowhere. All the remarkable things in life don't just land in our lap because we want them to. They happen because we take positive steps toward making it happen.

Acting doesn't require big steps. If your vision and purpose involve you starting a business, you can take lots of small steps, like thinking of a business name, searching online for premises or a domain name, speaking to a mentor and getting advice from an accountant. These little steps, taken one after another, compound to create massive momentum towards your vision. Motivation results from action. The more steps you take, the more motivation you have to take more steps.

> **What most people don't understand is that passion is the result of action, not the cause of it.**
>
> - Mark Manson

When you pull away in your car, you don't immediately go from 0-100kms per hour. You start slowly, and it takes a while to get going. Once you're going, and the car moves up a gear, the energy needed to get to the next level is the same just to get moving. Finally, you're moving at 100km per hour, and it feels like the car is barely doing anything at all. It's the same with taking action to achieve your goals. The first few actions may feel like tough going, but small wins create momentum.

Take people who attend my studios for fitness classes. Joseph Pilates said, "after 10 sessions you will feel a difference, after 20, you'll see a difference, and after 30 sessions you will have a completely new body". We aren't asking you to attend your 30th session today, just your 1st. That momentum you create will open new doors, new opportunities where you would never have dreamed.

Something that will probably happen along the way is sometimes you'll get stuck. You'll have a difficult day, a bad week, or a bad month. Work or home will be overwhelming, and the last thing you want to do is take that action that will bring you closer to your vision. When this happens, you have three options. Do nothing. Do something. Or get help. It is best not to do nothing! Anything you can do to keep your momentum going will be helpful. You never know when you will have your next breakthrough!

We also have to enjoy the journey! Plans are supposed to unfold bit by bit. Be patient, have faith, and celebrate the small wins.

The most fulfilment in life comes from finding the answers yourself. Don't wait for someone else to spoon-feed you the answer. Be resourceful! Take responsibility for yourself and your life and go out and find those answers. There is an abundance of freely available information on the internet which will give you what you need.

Most of the people I work with already know the answers. They know that the key to weight loss is to reduce food intake and increase exercise. They know they need a new job, or to put more effort into their relationship, or to stop wasting money. One way to speed up the pace you act is to add accountability. It just makes everything happen faster. It can also be the difference between taking action and sitting around doing nothing. On the flipside, quite often we don't know the answers. All we can do is take the next step and believe that everything will unfold as it should.

Talking to a friend who's on a similar journey as you can be so massively motivating (and can increase your Connectedness). Meanwhile, talking to an expert coach who has been through the journey with many others before you can help you avoid the pitfalls. This can challenge you to overcome the problems that arise. A good coach isn't there to tell you what to do. They help you come up with the right answers yourself, then support you on your journey.

Scott Capelin

Final Thoughts

Stop for a moment now and ask yourself these questions:

- Looking back on this book, what is one thing that has stood out to me?
- What is one action step I can take today to make a positive improvement in my life?
- What are my top three values in life?
- Where am I doing really well in life right now?
- What are three things I am truly grateful for in my life?
- If I had to set one goal right now, what would it be?
- What gives me a powerful sense of purpose in life?
- If I had to make one substantial change in my life, what would it be?
- What are my natural gifts or talents?

I hope you can see how these 7 steps to mastering your mindset work together to increase the amount of passion and inspiration in your life. I encourage you to ponder the topics presented in this book, take with you what you find useful, question the areas you're not sure about, and forget about anything you didn't find useful.

Personal development is an intimate journey that you take with yourself, and it often starts with an intuitive feeling that there is a better way to live this one life we are given. If you have an inkling that there is more waiting for you than you are currently experiencing, go out there and grab it!

> **Almost every succesful person begins with two beliefs: the future can be better than the present, and I have the power to make it so.**

About the Author

"I firmly believe that the universe directs us towards a place that we belong. I've had my fair share of ups and downs, and now I have a beautiful family and a thriving business and and I feel like I am exactly where I am supposed to be. If it was not for the hard times I've been through, I would not be where I am now, so I am grateful for them. I can see that everything really does happen for a reason"

~ Scott Capelin ~

Scott Capelin

A qualified wellness coach, nutritionist, International Best Selling Author, author, Business Graduate, and life coach, Scott Capelin comes to you having owned twelve successful businesses over a 20 year peri, with extensive business mentoring experience and over 25 years working with clients in the fitness industry and wellness arena.

By his own admission, however, Scott has also had his fair share of disappointment – losing one business, his livelihood and his family home while his wife was pregnant with their third child. Never one to give up, he worked to gain it all back, and more, within two years.

Seeing his role as helping others achieve a healthy, happy lifestyle through balancing family, fitness and finances, Scott Capelin is passionate about providing advice and encouragement as someone who has 'been there and done that!'

Fit to Flourish

Scott Capelin

Fit to Flourish

Scott Capelin

www.ingramcontent.com/pod-product-compliance
Lightning Source LLC
Chambersburg PA
CBHW070052120426
42742CB00048B/2481